Camilla Gryski's

Cat's Cradle

A Book of String Games

Illustrated by Tom Sankey

KIDS CAN PRESS

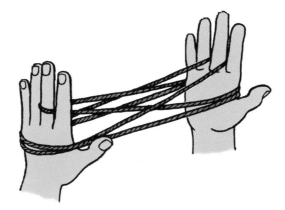

Chapter title string photograph by Steve Payne

The material in this book originally appeared in *Cat's Cradle*, *Owl's Eyes* and
Many Stars and More String Games.

Kids Can Press acknowledges the financial support of the Government of Canada,
through the BPIDP, for our publishing activity.

Published in Canada by	Published in the U.S. by
Kids Can Press Ltd.	Kids Can Press Ltd.
29 Birch Avenue	2250 Military Road
Toronto, ON M4V 1E2	Tonawanda, NY 14150

www.kidscanpress.com

Printed and bound in China
This book is limp sewn with drawn-on cover.

CM PA 01 0 9 8 7 6 5 4 3

Canadian Cataloguing in Publication Data
Gryski, Camilla, 1948–

Camilla Gryski's cat's cradle : a book of string games

ISBN 1-55337-090-2

1. String figures — Juvenile literature. I. Sankey, Tom. II. Title.
III. Title: Cat's cradle.

GV1218.S8G75 2001   j793.9   C00-933013-5

Contents

Introduction

When I was young, I played Cat's Cradle with my friends. It was the only string game I knew. Then when I began to study string figures, I learned different ways to make each Cat's Cradle pattern. I even learned to play Cat's Cradle all by myself.

The game of Cat's Cradle probably travelled from Asia to Europe with the tea trade in the seventeenth century. We know that children in England played Cat's Cradle as early as 1782, because a writer named Charles Lamb talked about weaving "cat-cradles" with his friends when he was at school.

In most Cat's Cradle figures, you can see X's and straight strings. When you play the game with two people, one person holds the figure while the other picks up the X's and takes them over, under or between the straight strings. The players take turns holding the figure and picking up the X's to move to the next step. There are many different ways to pick up the X's, so keep experimenting — that's the fun of the game.

I learned to play Solo Cat's Cradle from a book of Japanese string games. It's harder to play Cat's Cradle by yourself, so don't try to learn all the steps at once. Learn a couple of steps really well, then gradually add steps until you know them all. Along the way, you can ask a friend to play with you. Because of the way the strings cross over one another, you can sometimes turn your Solo Cat's Cradle into a two-person game — and sometimes you can't. Solo Cat's Cradle is very impressive, so don't give up too easily.

Whether you're playing with a friend or by yourself, Happy Cat's Cradling!

AS YOU PLAY, MAKE SURE YOU ARE HOLDING YOUR STRINGS SECURELY BEFORE YOUR PARTNER TAKES HIS OR HER HANDS OUT OF THE FIGURE.

About the String

The Inuit used sinew or a leather thong to make their string figures. Other peoples farther south made twine from the inside of bark. We are told that Tikopian children in the Pacific Islands area preferred fibre from the hibiscus tree, although they would use a length of fishing line if it was handy. Some people even used human hair, finely braided.

Fortunately, you don't have to go out into the woods or cut your hair to get a good string for making string figures. You can use ordinary white butcher's string knotted together at the ends. Macrame cord also works quite well, because it is thicker than string. A thicker string loop will show off your string figures better.

Dressmaker's supply stores sell nylon cord, usually by the metre or foot. This kind of cord is probably the best, and because it is woven, not plied or twisted, it won't crease. It can be joined without a knot. A knot in your string loop can cause tangles, and figures that move won't go smoothly if there is a knot in the way.

How to Make Your String

You need about two metres (six feet) of string or cord, so that your string loop will measure one metre (three feet) when it is joined. This is a standard size. If this length seems uncomfortably long, a shorter string is fine for most of the figures.

The string can either be tied or melted together.

To tie your string

You need a knot that won't slip, so a square knot is best.

1 Lay the right end of the string across the left end.

2 Put this right end under the left string to tie the first part of the knot.

3 Lay the new left end across the new right end.

4 Put this new left end under the new right string and tighten the knot.

5 Trim the ends to make the knot neat.

To melt your string

If the cord is nylon or some other synthetic fibre, you can melt the ends together. Joining the string takes practice, and it has to be done quickly, while the cord is hot. You will probably need some help, so please do this with an adult.

1 Hold the ends of the string near each other, about one to two centimetres (one-half an inch) above a candle flame. If the ends are not melting at all, they are too far away from the flame. They will singe if you are holding them too close.

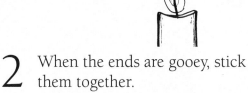

2 When the ends are gooey, stick them together.

3 Count to five to let them cool, then roll them between your fingers to smooth the join.

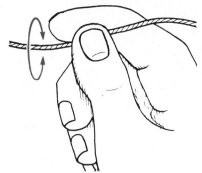

You have now made your "play string," or "ayahaak," as the Inuit call it.

Terminology

There's a Special Language

A long time ago, people made lists of the names of string figures or brought back drawings of the finished patterns. Some even kept the string pattern itself, fastened to a piece of paper. But once a string figure is finished, it is almost impossible to tell just how it was made.

We can learn and teach each other string figures today because, in 1898, two anthropologists, Dr. A.C. Haddon and Dr. W.H.R. Rivers, invented a special language to describe the way string figures are made. Haddon and Rivers developed their special language to record all the steps it took to make the string figures they learned in the Torres Straits. Then, other anthropologists used this same language, or a simpler version of it, when they wanted to remember the string figures they saw in their travels.

The language used in this book to describe the making of the figures is similar to that used by Haddon and Rivers. The loops and the strings have names, and there are also names for some of the basic positions and moves.

About Loops

When the string goes around your finger or thumb, it makes a **loop**. The loops take their names from their location on your hands: **thumb loop, index loop, middle finger loop, ring finger loop, little finger loop**.

If you move a loop from one finger to another, it gets a new name: a loop that was on your thumb but is now on your little finger is a new little finger loop.

Each loop has a **near string** — the one nearer (or closer) to you — and a **far string** — the one farther from you.

If there are two loops on your thumb or finger, one is the **lower loop** — the one near the base of your thumb or finger — and the other is the **upper loop** — the one near the top of your thumb or finger. Don't get these loops mixed up, and be sure to keep them apart.

About Making the Figures

As you make the figures in this book, you will be weaving the strings of the loops on your fingers. Your fingers or thumbs can go over or under the strings to pick up one or more strings, then go back to the basic position.

Sometimes you may **drop** or **release** a loop from your fingers.

It takes a little while to get used to holding your hands so that the strings don't drop off your fingers. If you accidentally drop a loop or a string, it is best to start all over again.

Now go and get your string — let's begin!

NAMES OF THE STRINGS

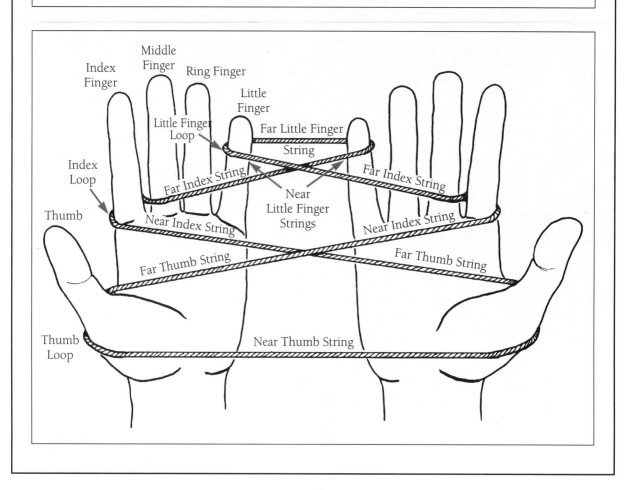

The Basic Position

Your hands begin in the **basic position** for most string figures and usually return to the basic position after each move.

1 Your hands are parallel, the palms are facing each other, and your fingers are pointing up.

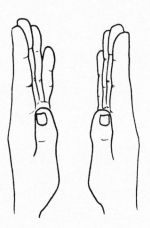

The hands in some of the pictures are not in the basic position. The hands are shown with the palms facing you so that you can see all the strings clearly.

Position 1

1 With your hands in the basic position, hang the loop of string on your thumbs. Stretch your hands as far apart as you can to make the string loop tight.

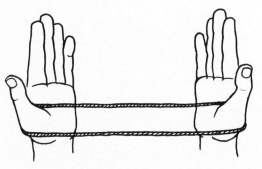

2 Pick up the far thumb string with your little fingers. The string that goes across the palm of your hand is called the **palmar string**.

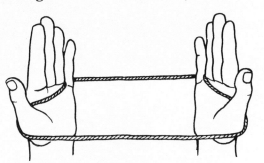

Opening A

Many string figures begin with **Opening A**.

1 Put the string loop on your fingers in Position 1.

2 With your right index finger, pick up, from below, the palmar string on your left hand and return to the basic position, pulling this string on the back of your index finger as far as it will go.

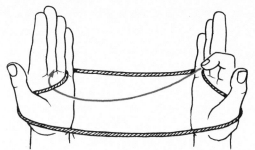

3 With your left index finger, pick up the right palmar string from below, in between the strings of the loop that goes around your right index finger. Return to the basic position, again pulling out the palmar string as far as it will go.

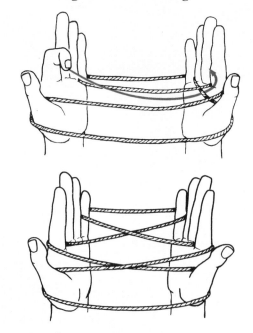

To Navaho a Loop

When you have two loops on your thumb or finger, a lower loop and an upper loop, you **Navaho** these loops by lifting the lower loop — with the thumb and index finger of your opposite hand, or with your teeth — up over the upper loop and over the tip of your finger or thumb.

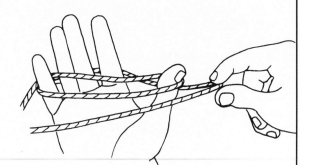

You can also Navaho a loop by tipping down your thumb or finger, letting the lower loop slip off, then straightening up your thumb or finger again.

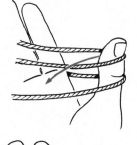

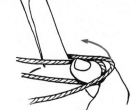

To Share a Loop

Sometimes you will **share a loop** between two fingers or a finger and your thumb. You use your opposite index finger and thumb to pull out the loop so that the other finger or thumb will fit into the loop as well.

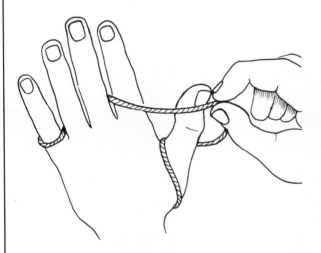

To Extend a Figure

Sometimes the strings may be woven and a figure may be finished, but it needs to be **extended** by pulling the hands apart or by turning or twisting the hands in a certain way. Extending the figure makes a tangle of strings magically turn into a beautiful pattern.

To Take the Figure Apart

Always take the figures apart gently — tugging creates knots. If the figure has top and bottom straight strings that frame the pattern, pull these apart and the pattern will dissolve.

Getting a String or Strings

When the instructions tell you to **get** a string or strings, your finger or thumb goes under that string, picks up that string on its back (the back of your finger or thumb is the side with the fingernail), then returns to the basic position, carrying the string with it. The instructions will tell you if you are to use your fingers or thumb to pick up the strings in a different way.

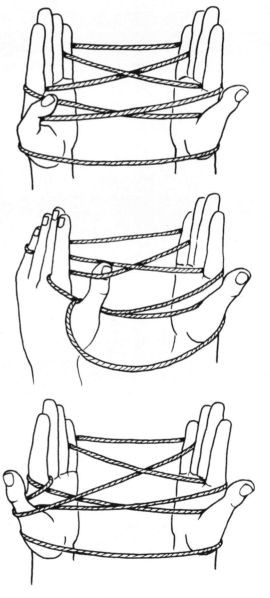

Cat's Cradle

(With a Friend)

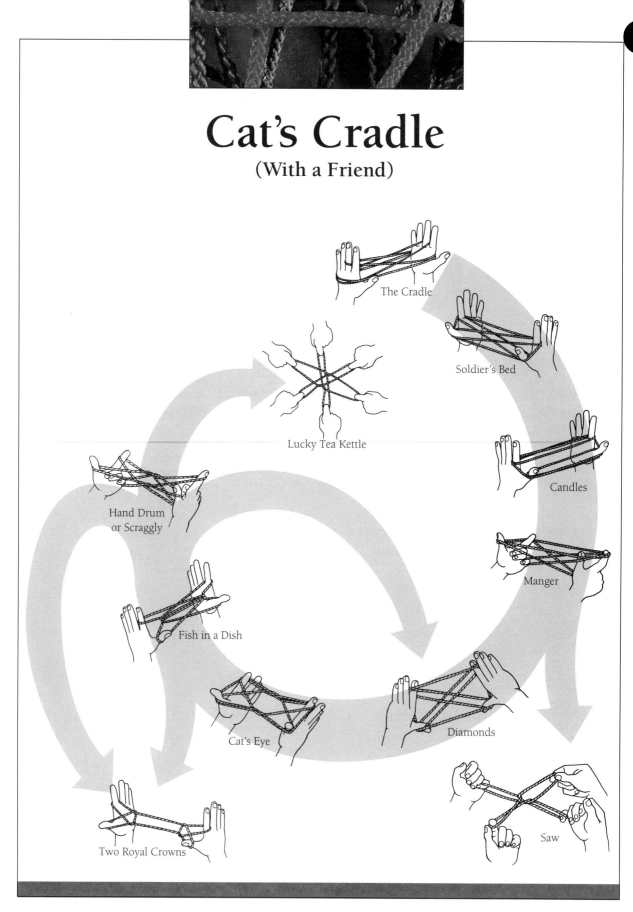

The Cradle

Soldier's Bed

Lucky Tea Kettle

Candles

Hand Drum or Scraggly

Manger

Fish in a Dish

Cat's Eye

Diamonds

Two Royal Crowns

Saw

1 The Cradle

A makes the Cradle

1 Put the string loop around the backs of the fingers (but not the thumb) of each hand.

2 Your right index finger and thumb pick up the near string of the loop around your left hand and wrap it once around your left hand. The string comes out between your left index finger and thumb.

3 Your left index finger and thumb pick up the near string of the loop around your right hand and wrap it once around your right hand. Make sure you always pick up the **near** string. One near and one far string wrapped around will give you tangled candles later on.

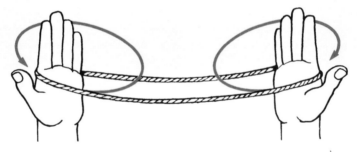

4 Now complete as in Opening A, using your middle fingers.

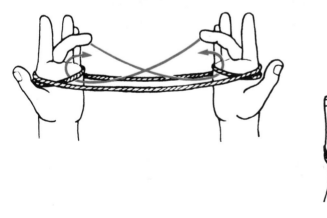
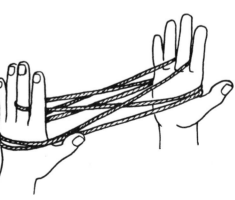

2 Cradle to Soldier's Bed

B makes the Soldier's Bed

1 Your index fingers and thumbs take hold of the X's at the sides of the figure.

2 Pull the X's out to the sides.

3 Push the X's down and take them under the long side framing strings at the bottom of the figure. Now turn your index fingers and thumbs up.

4 Separate your index fingers and thumbs to make the Bed.

3 Soldier's Bed to Candles

A makes Candles

1 Your index fingers and thumbs take the long X's.

2 Pull the X's up, out past the framing strings of the figure.

3 Push the X's down and under the straight framing strings. Now turn your index fingers and thumbs up.

4 Separate your index fingers and thumbs to make Candles.

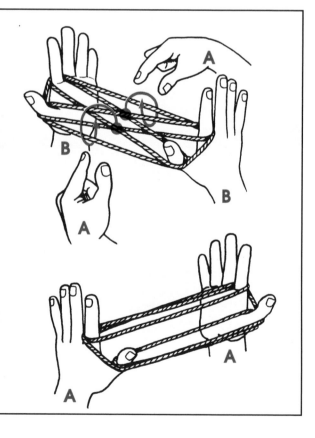

4 Candles to Manger

B makes the Manger

1 Use your left little finger, face up, like a hook, to get the far thumb candle string and pull it across the figure out past the far index strings. Hang on to this string.

2 Use your right little finger, face up, like a hook, to get the near index candle string and pull it across the figure out past the near thumb strings.

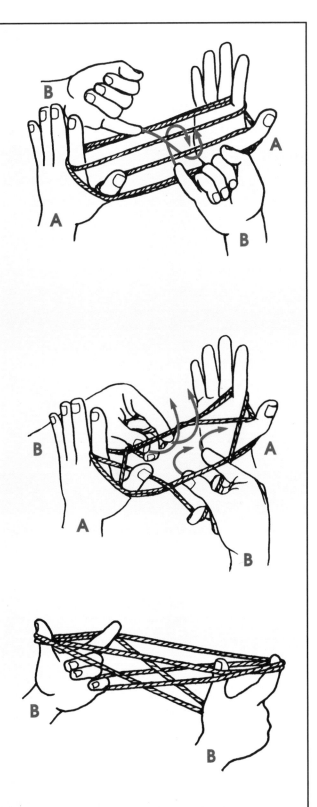

3 Now your right index finger and thumb go down into the string triangle between the framing strings of the figure and the string held by your right little finger. In the same way, your left index finger and thumb go down into the string triangle held by your left little finger.

4 Your index fingers and thumbs go under, then pick up on their backs the straight framing strings of the figure.

5 Continue to hold the little finger strings securely and separate your index fingers and thumbs to make the Manger.

You can end the game here by making the Saw (figure 5). If you want to continue, go on to make Diamonds (figure 6).

5 | Manger to Saw

A makes the Saw and ends the game

1 A takes the top framing side strings of the figure.

2 B drops the strings from his/her index fingers and thumbs but continues to hold the little finger loops.

3 Now you and your friend take turns pulling on your string loops to make the strings saw back and forth.

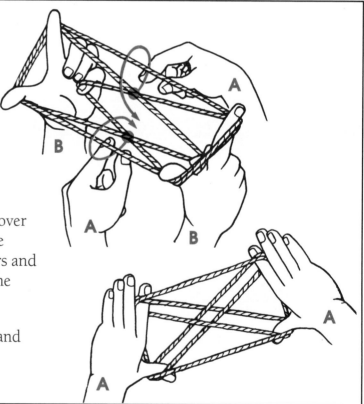

6 | Manger to Diamonds

A makes Diamonds

1 Your index fingers and thumbs take the long X's at the sides of the figure.

2 Pull the X's out, then up.

3 Now take the X's across and over the top framing strings of the figure and point your index fingers and thumbs down into the centre of the figure.

4 Separate your index fingers and thumbs to make Diamonds.

7 Diamonds to Cat's Eye

B makes Cat's Eye

1 Your index fingers and thumbs take the long X's.

2 Pull them up and out past the framing strings of the figure.

3 Now push them down and under the straight framing strings, and turn your index fingers and thumbs up.

4 Separate your index fingers and thumbs to make Cat's Eye.

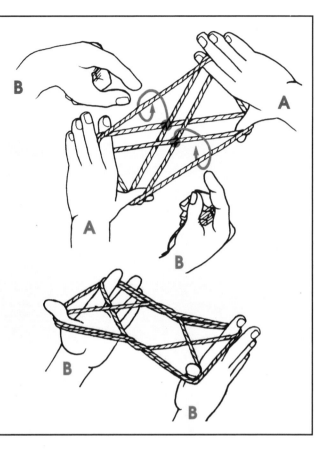

8 Cat's Eye to Fish in a Dish

A makes Fish in a Dish

1 Your index fingers and thumbs go down into the loops held by B's index fingers and thumbs, and pinch the sides of the central diamond where they meet the framing strings.

2 Turn your index fingers and thumbs up into the large central diamond of the figure.

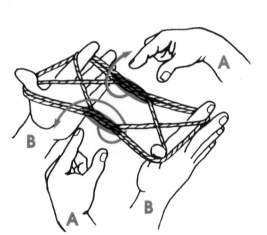

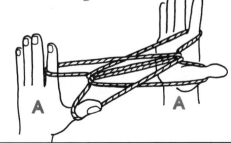

3 Separate your index fingers and thumbs to make Fish in a Dish.

You can end the game here by making Two Royal Crowns (figure 9). If you want to continue, go on to make Hand Drum or Scraggly (figure 10).

17

9 Fish in a Dish to Two Royal Crowns

B makes Two Royal Crowns and ends the game

Your index fingers and thumbs take the long X's and pull them out to the sides to make the Crowns.

---

10 Fish in a Dish to Hand Drum or Scraggly

B makes the Hand Drum or Scraggly

This time, the X's are on the outside and the straight strings are in the centre.

1 Each little finger takes the straight central string nearest to it and pulls it out past the X's. Hang on to these strings. There is now a central diamond framed by the X's.

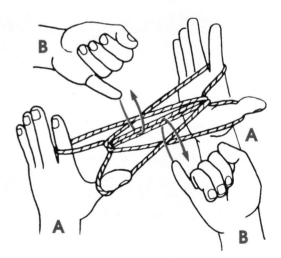

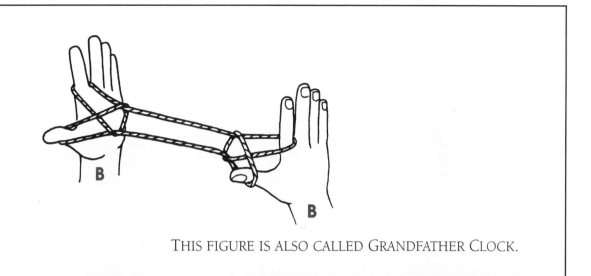

THIS FIGURE IS ALSO CALLED GRANDFATHER CLOCK.

2 Now your index fingers and thumbs take the X's as usual.

3 Still holding the little finger strings, turn your index fingers and thumbs up into the central diamond.

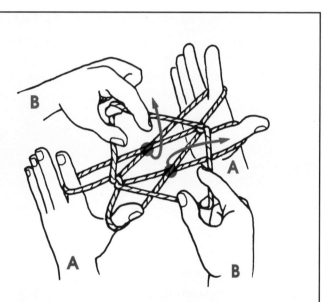

4 Separate your index fingers and thumbs to complete the Hand Drum.

You can end the game here by making Two Royal Crowns (figure 11) or the Lucky Tea Kettle (figure 12). If you want to continue, go on to make Diamonds (figure 13).

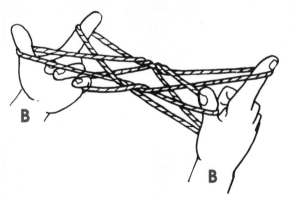

11 Hand Drum to Two Royal Crowns

B makes the Crowns and ends the game

Release the loops from your little
fingers to make Two Royal Crowns.

12 Hand Drum to the Lucky Tea Kettle

It takes three people to make the Lucky Tea Kettle. Go and call a friend. In Japan, they end the game this way. Each person takes two loops of the Hand Drum figure.

1 B is holding the Drum and keeps the loops on his/her index fingers.

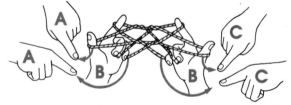

2 A takes the loops from B's left little finger and thumb.

3 C takes the loops from B's right little finger and thumb.

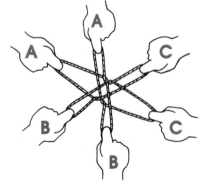

This is the Hibachi on which the Lucky Tea Kettle is put to boil. But, according to a Japanese fairy tale, the Lucky Tea Kettle is no ordinary tea kettle. It is, in fact, a talented badger tea kettle named Bumbuku-Chagama. When the kettle becomes a badger, a head with two bright eyes looks out of the spout, and four brown hairy paws and a bushy tail appear. You can imagine the clatter and clang as the Lucky Tea Kettle, complaining loudly, jumps off the fire!

To end the game, the three people holding the strings of the Hibachi shout "Chan-garagara!" which is the noise of the tea kettle jumping off the fire. Then they all let go of their strings at once. The one left holding the strings loses the game.

13 Hand Drum to Diamonds

A makes Diamonds

First you have to find the X's. The figure has four upper loops held by B's index fingers and thumbs, and two lower loops held by B's little fingers. The strings that make the X's run up from B's little fingers.

1 Put your index fingers and thumbs from each side of the figure into the space between the upper and lower loops. Your index fingers and thumbs are touching the strings of both little finger loops. Slide your index fingers and thumbs towards each other along the strings of the little finger loops until they close on the strings that lace together in the middle of each side of the figure.

When you pull these strings out to the sides, the X's should come free, leaving only two straight framing strings.

2 Your index fingers and thumbs pull the X's out to the sides.

3 Now take the X's towards each other over the framing strings.

4 Turn your index fingers and thumbs down into the centre space of the figure.

5 Separate your index fingers and thumbs to make Diamonds.

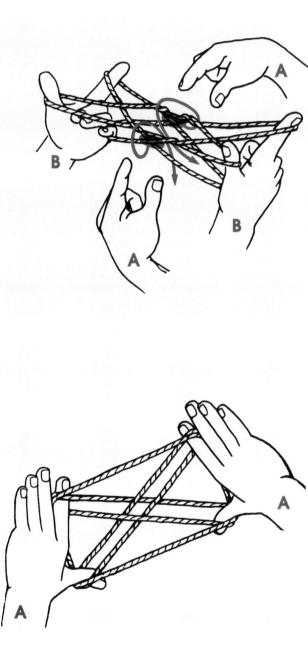

Mystery Figures

Now that you have played Cat's Cradle to the end, you are ready to experiment with some mystery figures. These are variations of the moves you made the first time around, but you will see that the results are quite different.

Cat's Eye Mystery Figure

This figure is a bit tricky, so you'll probably have to look at the pictures.

First, follow the instructions from the beginning of the Cradle (figure 1) to the end of Cat's Eye (figure 7).

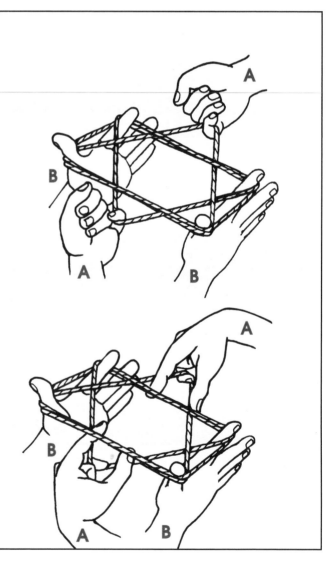

Now your little fingers pull out the strings that make the sides of the central diamond, just where they lace through the side framing strings.

What happens when your index fingers and thumbs turn down and under the framing strings, then up into the centre of the figure?

Fish in a Dish Mystery Figures

There are two possible variations.

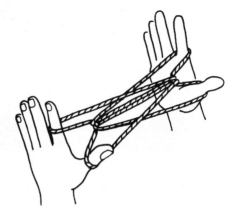

1 First, follow the instructions from the Cradle (figure 1) to the end of Fish in a Dish (figure 8).

Now see what happens when you take the long X's down into the centre of the figure between the two straight central strings.

2 To do the second Fish in a Dish Mystery Figure, again follow the instructions to the end of figure 8.

What figure do you get when you take the X's up into the centre of the figure from below, between the two straight central strings?

Hand Drum Mystery Figure

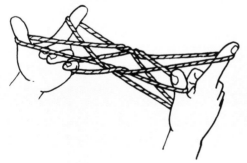

First, follow the instructions from the Cradle (figure 1) to the end of Hand Drum (figure 10). When you have the Hand Drum, you will need to find the X's, as you did at the beginning of figure 13. If you've forgotten where they are, read instruction 1 for figure 13 again.

Now see what happens when you take the X's down under the framing strings and up into the centre of the figure.

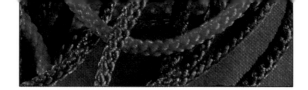

Solo Cat's Cradle

(All by Yourself)

1 The Cradle

1 Do Opening A, picking up the palmar strings with your middle fingers.

2 Cradle to Soldier's Bed

1 Turn your hands so that the palms are facing you. Put all your fingers down into the thumb loops and throw the thumb loops over the backs of your hands. The hand loops should be lower than the middle finger and little finger loops.

2 Turn your hands so that the palms are facing away from you. Put all your fingers, including your little fingers, but not your thumbs, down into the little finger loops, and throw the little finger loops towards you over your fingers and your thumbs.

You now have loops on your middle fingers, and the hand loops cross over on the backs of your hands.

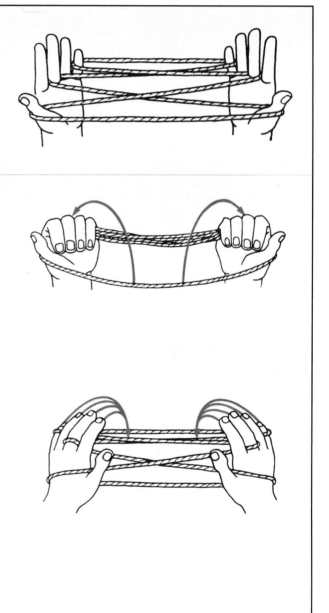

3 Your thumbs get the near middle finger strings.

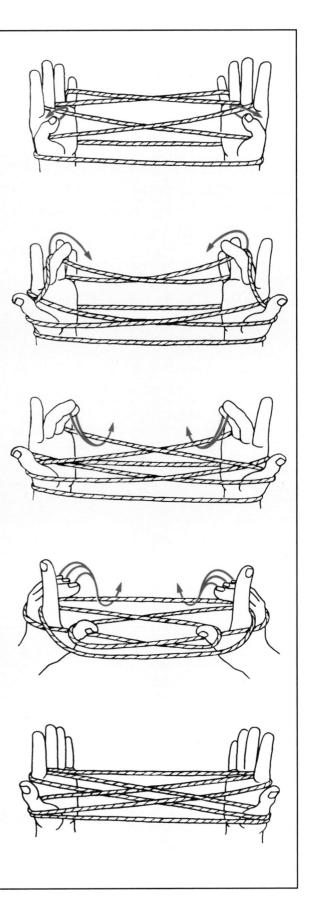

4 Your middle fingers drop their loops.

5 Tip your ring fingers and middle fingers down under the strings that lie between your ring fingers and little fingers. Let these strings slide over the backs of these fingers to lie in the space between your index fingers and middle fingers.

6 Tip your little, ring and middle fingers down under the far string of the hand loops. Let this string slide over the backs of these fingers to also lie in the space between your middle fingers and index fingers. This is the Soldier's Bed.

3 Soldier's Bed to Candles

1 Take your left hand out of its loops.

2 Put your left thumb back up into the thumb loops from below, near your right thumb.

3 Put your left index finger back up into the index loops from below, near your right index finger.

4 When you separate your hands to return to the basic position, you will see that the crosses have come undone — giving you Candles.

4 Candles to Diamonds

1 Your little fingers come towards you, over the strings, to get the far thumb candle string and return.

2 Your thumbs drop their loops.

3 Look for the near straight string that runs from index finger to index finger. Your thumbs go under this string, then over all the strings of the index loops to get the near little finger strings and return. Each thumb now has two loops.

4 Your little fingers drop their loops.

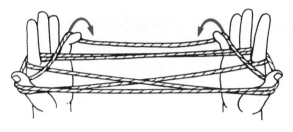

5 Hook your index fingers down towards you, over the near index strings, and keep these strings in the hooks of your index fingers while you let the other loops slide off your index fingers.

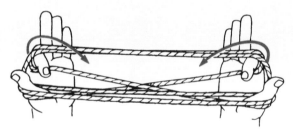

6 Straighten up your index fingers without twisting the index loops. There's now one loop on each index finger. (What a tidy Navaho!)

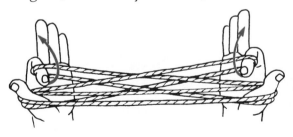

7 Look for the straight far thumb string, which runs from thumb to thumb. Your index fingers tip down to get this string and return to make Diamonds.

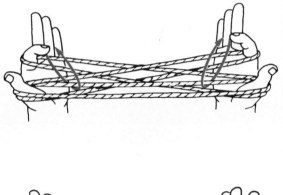

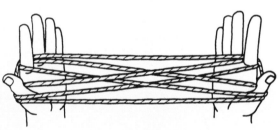

5 Diamonds to Cat's Eye

1 Your little fingers go up into the index loops.

2 Your little fingers bring, on their backs, the crossed far index strings out under the straight far index string.

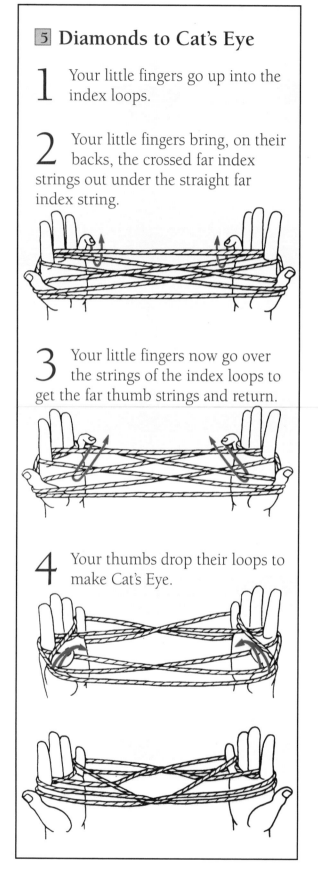

3 Your little fingers now go over the strings of the index loops to get the far thumb strings and return.

4 Your thumbs drop their loops to make Cat's Eye.

6 Cat's Eye to Hand Drum or Scraggly

1 Your thumbs go up into the little finger loops. Move your thumbs towards each other until they can catch, on their backs, the diagonal strings that run from your index fingers to lace through the far little finger strings. Your thumbs return under the other strings to their usual position, carrying these strings with them as new thumb loops.

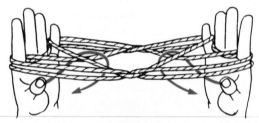

2 Your index fingers now hook down over the straight near little finger string. As they return to their usual position, the old double index loops will slip off your index fingers and this straight string will curve around your index fingers to become the far string of the new index loops.

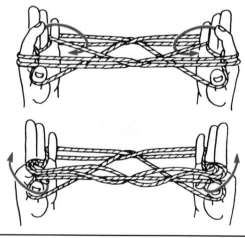

If you are standing up, please sit down, because you need a lap for the next step.

3 Each little finger has two loops: one ordinary loop, with a near and a far string; and one loop whose near string crosses your palm. Turn your hands so that the fingers are facing down, nearly touching your lap. Gently take your little fingers out of their double loops. When you release them, the near little finger strings that crossed your palm will become near index strings, leaving the other ordinary little finger loops lying on your lap.

4 Use your little fingers like hooks to catch from below, and hold, these little finger loops. Return your hands to the basic position. This is the Hand Drum or Scraggly.

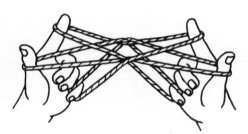

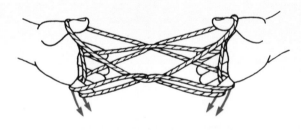

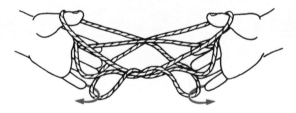

7 Hand Drum to Manger

You have loops on your index fingers, loops on your thumbs and loops held in the hooks of your little fingers.

1 Your thumbs get the near index strings and return. You have shared the index loops with your thumbs.

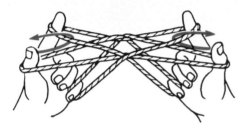

2 Your index fingers, without losing their loops, get the far thumb strings to share the thumb loops with your index fingers.

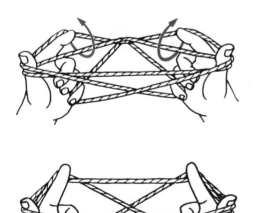

8 Manger to Cradle

Now you are elegantly going to return to the beginning so that, if you wish, you can start all over again.

1 Put your middle, ring and little fingers, with their loops, up into the large shared thumb/index loops and let these loops slide down around your wrists. You now have double wrist loops and little finger loops.

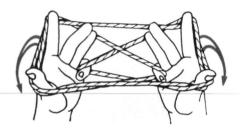

2 Your thumbs get the near little finger strings.

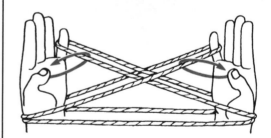

3 Do Opening A with your middle
fingers.

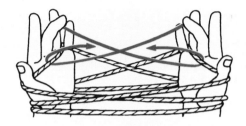

5 When you separate your hands
and return them to the basic
position, you will be back where
you started, ready for applause, or
ready to start all over again.

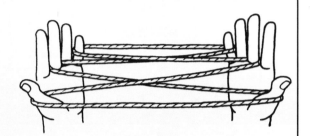

4 Now press the fingers of each
hand tightly together so that
the thumb, middle finger and little
finger loops do not slip off. Put your
hands palm to palm and turn your
fingers down to let the wrist loops
slide off your wrists and hands.

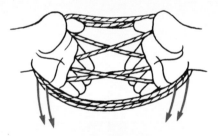

About the Author

Camilla Gryski has written many books for children, including *Cat's Cradle*, *Owl's Eyes*, which won an ALA Notable book award, and *Hands On, Thumbs Up*, which won the Rountables Information Book Award. Camilla lives in Toronto with her husband, two sons, two cats, and spends her spare time reading, making jewellery and...juggling!

Also by Camilla Gryski

Boondoggle: Making Bracelets with Plastic Lace
Camilla Gryski's Favourite String Games
Friendship Bracelets
Let's Play: Traditional Games of Childhood